What Kids are Saying About Liking Myself

"I like the book called 'Liking MySelf.' It helps me when I need it most. What I liked most was when you layed down and felt like you were somewhere else." —Elicia

"I thought it was very relaxing to know that I could control my own thoughts and choices." —Danielle

"I really enjoyed the unit on how to express my feelings. Now I can control my feelings of anger and embarrassment. Also, now I know how to take deep breaths before taking a test or doing an act in a school play."　　　—Stella

"I like Chapter 2 'Feeling' the best. Because I have read this book I have learned a very important thing. To express your feelings, you must not blame others. I have become able to express my thinking better than before, and I like myself better now. I have become gentle. I used to lie, but now I don't."　　　—Akiko, Japan

What Grown-ups are Saying About Liking Myself

"Liking Myself is an encouraging book for young people ages 5 to 11, offering advice on how to handle oneself when feeling depressed, upset, or overwhelmed. Blank spaces amid the hand-lettered pages and black-and-white, sketch-style illustrations encourage young people to write or draw their reactions to particular scenarios. The result is a valuable resource for building self-esteem and emotional stability."

—Midwest Book Review

"Liking Myself made me feel a million times better about myself. It helped me get rid of negativity and appreciate the little things in life!"

—Amazon reviewer

"A great little book to read with kids. Very helpful when working with 5-9 year-olds."

—Child Psychologist

"Liking Myself helps children find and restore their dignity."

—Michelle Brenner, Conflict Resolution Consultant in Family, Community, Government and Workplace, Sydney, Australia

"There are no adequate words to tell you how fantastic and helpful this book is."

"Liking Myself emphasizes that assertiveness is not aggression, and that teaching children to be strong and self-confident individuals gives them a head start toward a positive attitude for success in later life."

"This fun, happy, positive book is very enjoyable and rewarding to read through and discuss with your child."

What Grown-ups are Saying About
Liking Myself and The Mouse, the Monster and Me

"These books are delightful in their innocence, healthy in their advice, empowering in their message. I wish I'd grown up with them and their message."

—Senator John Vasconcellos, Emeritus Dean of the California Legislature

"These books are fantastic. I really enjoyed reading them myself, and I intend to use them in my work with juvenile offenders. Many read at the 3rd and 4th grade levels, and, unfortunately many do not like themselves."

—David, Parole Agent, Department of Youth Authority, Los Angeles, CA

"Parents can confidently provide these books to their children with full assurance that they contain the values and prescriptions for positive behavior."

—The Behavior Therapist Journal

"These books are enormously useful! Kids will like them. So will the adults who read them to kids. Everyone will grow."

—Dr. Sid Simon, Professor Emeritus at University of Massachusetts, author of Values Clarification.

"These books are positive, brief, and produced in a very interesting manner. Elementary school counselors and teachers can certainly use these practical books effectively with their students. Individual children can also benefit from them."

—*The Personnel and Guidance Journal*

"Young and old will benefit from both these cheerful little books. The young will especially benefit, however, if the adult reading with them is neither mouse nor monster."

—*School Social Work Journal*

Other Books by Pat Palmer

for young readers
The Mouse, the Monster, and Me
I Wish I Could Hold Your Hand
Teen Esteem

for adults (Japan)
Making Dreams Come True
A Primer on Love
Be a Happy Person
Anger Can Be Good for You

Liking Myself

by Pat Palmer, Ed.D.

www.upliftpress.com

Liking Myself

Copyright ©2009 by Pat Palmer
Revised with Louise Hart Ed.D.
All Rights Reserved
ISBN: 978-0-9622834-2-0

www.booksurge.com

Download the teacher's guide at www.upliftpress.com
Uplift Press, Oakland, CA
888-415-3414
admin@upliftpress.com

Hand-lettering and illustrations by Betty Shondeck
Typefaces: Hoefler Text, Kidprint

Liking Myself

Myself

By Pat Palmer, Ed. D.

Illustrated &
Handlettered By Betty L Shondeck

This book is dedicated to my children,

Penny and Betsy,

and to the child in each of us.

To the Young Reader

This book is yours for fun. It is full
of ideas, exercises and questions for you.
It is full of warm thoughts and love.
Ask your parents to read it with you.

Enjoy this book.
Enjoy yourself.
Enjoy being You!

Table of Contents

Liking Yourself

Part 1

It is OK
to like yourself
and be
your own good
friend.

To be a good friend to yourself,
do something nice for yourself like:

Play with a kitten...

Walk a dog...

Sing...

Bake cookies

Draw a picture...

... Whistle...

Play the piano...

..... Dance...

Climb a tree...

.. Smile...

Call a friend.

4

Write down or draw your _favorite_ things to do.

Do one nice thing each day as a
special gift to yourself.

Being a good friend to yourself means that:

...you can (STOP) doing something you don't like,

...you don't have to like everybody,

...everybody doesn't have to like you,

...you can rest when you are tired.

Often,
doing what others want is important.

Doing what `you` want is also important.

Being a good friend to yourself means...
...you can say nice things to yourself.

What a nice smile!

Write down or draw some nice things you can think or say about yourself.

Also, being a good friend to yourself means...
that it is |OK| to think about the things
you can do.

Write down or draw some of the things you can do.
(Don't worry if you're not "super-good." Nobody's Perfect!)

When you hear yourself saying mean things to yourself say, " STOP "!

Replace the mean thought with one of the nice things about you.

Say to yourself, "I am lovable and valuable," every time you walk through a door...

enter a car...

I am lovable and valuable!

PET SHOP

come to a stop sign...

STOP

Do this for two weeks,

... and ...

you will <u>feel</u> lovable and valuable!

Get some exercise every day to keep your body happy.

running

jumping

swimming

bicycling

hiking

Playing tag

baseball

skating

Write down or draw the kinds of exercises you like to do.

Keeping your body happy helps to keep the rest of you happy.

Liking yourself and being your own good friend helps you to like other people and be a good friend to them.

It is fun to give other people a treat, such as...

...scratching their backs...
(the way you like it, too!)

you bake Good cookies!

...sharing your favorite cookie...

...telling them nice things you like about them.

...giving them turns on your bike...

Share the good parts of you with others!

Enjoy being <u>you</u> right now!

Clap your hands...

Give yourself a hug...

Smile at yourself....

Be happy to be <u>you</u>!

... Now ...

Take some time

to go over what you have learned
about

♥ liking yourself ♥

before you go on to the next part of the book.

14

Part 2

Feelings

Feelings are good friends.

Feelings let us know...
   what is happening,
   what we want,
   what is important to us.

glad
happy
feeling good
ok
so-so
unhappy
sad
mad

Feelings are like a thermometer.

Pay attention to your feelings inside of you.
They tell you that you are...

sad

lonely

angry

glad

scared

hungry

cold

happy

Listen to your feelings. They tell you when you
need to take care of yourself, like finding a friend
if you feel lonely, crying if you feel sad, singing
and smiling if you feel happy, and acting frisky
if you feel good.

We can pretend not to feel, but we still have feelings anyway. Below are some strong feelings that everyone has once in awhile. Put a check (✓) by the ones you have felt.

___ I feel _lonesome_.   ___ I love baby animals.

___ I am all alone and _scared_.   ___ I feel _sad_.

___ I feel silly.   ___ I _like_ to swing

___ I _like_ my best friend.   ___ Sometimes I feel _helpless_.

___ When I am _tired_ I feel _down_.   ___ Sometimes I get _mad_ at mother.

___ Circuses are _exciting_!   ___ Playing ball is _fun_

If someone you love is hurt, leaves, or dies, being full of pain and grief is OK.

Boys and girls, ...

men and women... .

all have feelings ...

all need to be able to cry once in awhile.

It is OK to show your feelings!

Let yourself feel even the hard feelings, because...
holding them back 🖐 and ✍ pushing them 🔻down inside just

makes them stay . . . .
                and stay . . . .
                            and stay . . . .
                and keep hurting.
Let out the hurt feelings as fast as you can!
You don't need to hold on to them.
Let go of them so that they can leave.

Many men believe that to be manly,
a man shouldn't show any feelings.
So a big strong man isn't supposed to cry, to feel hurt,
to need help, or to feel lonesome.

Many people try to not let
others see who they really are.

If people pretend to not have feelings long
enough, one day they may not feel anything
any more, or at least they may not know what
feelings they are feeling.

Can you figure out what you are feeling
right now?

It is better to be sad and cry, if you feel
that way, than to hold it in and try
not to feel it.

...And... it is better to be happy and laugh,
if you feel that way,
to share it with others.

A lot of people like to pretend that some feelings aren't there.

A favorite one to pretend away is anger.

•Write down or draw some other feelings that people don't like to talk about.

... Anger is an OK feeling...

It tells you when someone is stomping on your flowers.

It tells you neat things about yourself, like...

...how you want to be treated...

...what you think is fair...

...things that you think are important...

- Write down or draw some of the things your anger helps you to know about yourself,...

...like what you need.

It's OK to ask for what you need.

Anger that is saved, and saved, and saved.

may explode into violence,

may cause you to be sick,

I have a tummy ache again

may lead you to hurt others,

either with words,

or with fists.

Inside ...

Your feelings help you to know what is right for <u>you</u>.

Feelings help you to decide what ...

...to do

...to say

...to try

...to like

...to not like.

Feelings <u>are</u> good friends!

··· Now ···

Take some time to go over what you have learned about

Feelings

before you go on to the next part of the book.

28

Feeling Talk

Part 3

Feeling talk is saying what you
feel or think
without hurting or upsetting others.

29

Talking about feelings hurts no one.
If I say, "I am angry,"
that doesn't hurt you.
If I say, "I am lonely,"
that lets you know me better.
The secret 🤚👂 is to start by saying,
"I think,"   "I feel,"   "I want."

I Think, I Feel, I Want Game

1. Ask a friend to be your partner.

2. Sit facing your friend.

3. Talk with your friend, starting each sentence with either "I think," "I feel," or "I want."

4. Share with your partner how it feels to talk starting each sentence with "I."

5. What happened? Did you learn anything new about your partner? Did you discover anything new about yourself? What kinds of things did you learn?

Another secret to good feeling talk is <u>not</u> to say to another person, • "<u>You</u> are … (dumb, stupid, mean)," • "<u>YOU</u> did it … ," or • "<u>YOU</u> make me mad."

When you are mad, talk about how <u>you feel</u> and maybe why you feel that way, but <u>not</u> about other people.

Calling others names makes <u>them</u> feel bad, or upset, or mad at you. What happens to <u>you</u> when someone calls you a name? How do you feel when someone gets mad at you?

Feeling words are good friends...
They help you to tell what is going on inside of you.
Here are some feeling words. Can you think of some more?

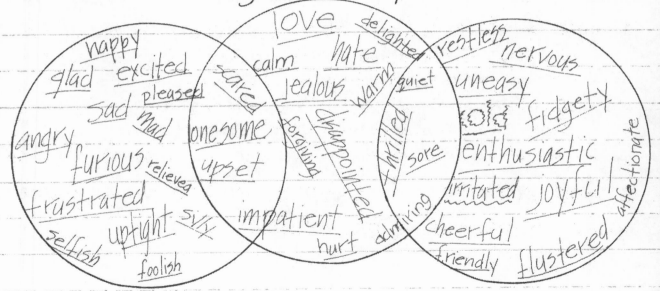

Feeling Talk Game

1. Ask a friend to play with you.
2. Stand facing each other.
3. Use feeling talk to act out (pretend) a time when:
   - One of you has just stepped on the other's toe.
   - One of you forgot to return a pencil.
   - One of you asks to borrow something and the other says "No."
   - One of you has just broken the other's bike.
   - One of you has just lost a favorite pet. It was hit by a car.

4. Add more real life times in which you would like to practice using Feeling Talk.

When you talk about a feeling no one has to do anything or say anything, unless they _want_ to.

...So, if your friend is late and you say, "I'm really upset. I've been waiting for 20 minutes for you and I'm mad." You feel better. Your friend knows that you are upset about being late. But you didn't call your friend "stupid" for being late.

When you talk about your feelings, no one needs to feel guilty, bad or punished. You are just talking about how _you_ feel, and what has happened to _you_.

Sometimes it feels scary to say your feelings to adults. It can help to practice feeling talk with people who are in charge. Practice with a friend. Pretend your friend is your mother, father, teacher, principal or another adult. Tell the pretend adult....

- How you feel about him or her.
- How you feel about something very important to you such as a sadness, something that hurts you that the adult does or says, a feeling of deep love, or a problem with a friend.
- That you think a rule is unfair or won't work.
- About a real life situation that is bothering you.

Remember to use feeling talk!

Sharing and Caring Game

1. Ask a friend or family member to be your partner.

2. Sit facing each other.

3. Take turns telling each other the things you like about <u>each other</u>.

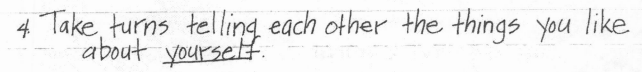

4. Take turns telling each other the things you like about <u>yourself</u>.

5. Be sure to listen to each other.

Everyone needs love.

Feeling talk is a way of talking about...

...loving

...feeling sad

...liking

...giving compliments

being angry

... sharing and caring...

I love you!

I like your smile!

I feel sad today

I'm really upset. I have been waiting...

NOW

Take some time
to go over what you have learned about

Feeling Talk

before you go on to the next part of the book.

Part 4

Allowing

You can be different from everyone else, and still be OK

Allow yourself to be human.
Humans have feelings.
Humans are warm and loving.
Sometimes even humans like to...

...climb trees...

slither through the jungle

roar roar like a lion...

baaaa like a sheep...

...or even mess things up...

weep like a weeping willow...

...jump like a kangaroo...

Being human is nice!

Allow yourself to be you...

to be...

rare...
beautiful...
individual...

1 of a kind award

unusual

opposite

...different
special...

Write down or draw some of the things about you that are special.

It is OK to be different!

The Difference Game

1. Sit down with your friend.

2. Tell the things about you that are different from your friend.

3. Ask your friend to tell you the things that are different from you.

4. Ask your friend the things he or she likes about you.

5. Tell what you like about your friend.

I really like your hair.

Allow yourself to make mistakes. Sometimes you may feel badly for making a mistake,... like forgetting to come home on time, or pulling out the bottom can in a supermarket and causing a crash, or forgetting to do something you were supposed to do.

<u>But</u>... the most important thing is to fix your mistakes! Help stack up the cans again! Be home on time today!

Allow yourself to think of mistakes as a way of learning how to do things better. Then, making a mistake can be OK. Also, remember that it is not fair to others or to yourself to use, "I made a mistake," as an <u>excuse</u> for being careless, or for not doing your job, or for hurting others.

• List a few mistakes that taught you something.

. . . Did you fix them?

Allow yourself to change your mind ...

You can become a doctor instead of a nurse ....

You can change your favorite color...

You can change your favorite game ...

...or movie

You can change your favorite game ...

or food ...

... or story...

48

You can decide to like yourself...
   instead of not liking yourself.

You can change your <u>mind</u>... or...
   <u>yourself</u>   anytime.

• Write down or draw <u>one</u> change <u>you</u> would like to work on.

Allow yourself to do things "just because."

You don't have to have a reason for everything.

You don't have to explain everything you do.

Having a "why" for everything isn't necessary.

Doing what you want to do is OK...

as long as ...

you don't hurt anyone...

or make them feel bad.

Allow yourself to be you. You don't have to pretend to be someone else ...or act like someone else... or copy someone else...or talk like someone else...or look like someone else.

You can relax and just be you!

Allowing yourself to be happy causes happy things to happen to you. Nice thoughts color your life happy colors. Being nice to yourself, being your own good friend, helps others to be nice to you, too, and to be your friend.

•Draw a picture of yourself with happy colors.

Being good and kind to yourself helps all
the people around you like __themselves__ and __you__!

• Draw your own smile and wear it!

Now...

Take some (time) to go over

what you have learned about...

Allowing

before going on to the next part of the book.

54

Part 5

Body Talk

Your body
talks
to you
all the time.
Learn how to listen!

Check your body right now.
- Do you take deep breaths?
- Do you slouch in your chair?
- Is your lower back tight?
- Is your stomach tight?
- Are your knees locked?
- Is your jaw tight?
- Is your fist clenched?
- Is your neck relaxed?
- Do you have a headache?
- Are your shoulders up high?
- Do you chew your fingers?

Take a few very deep breaths and

let go

of the tightness in your body.

Your body wears out faster when it is held tight.
Your body can get sick if it is held tight all the time.

Learn to listen to your body; check it out often,
and

let go

when it feels tight.

Letting Go Game

Directions: Find someone to read this to you. It should be read slowly with pauses after each sentence.

- Lie down on the floor with your eyes closed.
- Feel the floor holding up your body.
- Take a deep breath all the way down to your tummy.
- Slowly let it out.
- Take another deep breath and this time fill up your body and legs with air.
- Slowly empty out all the air. • Lie quietly for a few minutes, breathing slowly and deeply.
- Open your eyes, and sit up slowly.

Sunshine Game

Lie on the floor or a bed with your eyes closed. Be aware of your breathing. Take some deep breaths down into your belly. Let your body become very heavy.

Imagine a tiny, speck of light in your belly. Slowly let it expand. Very slowly it will fill your belly with light, energy and warmth. Gradually the light spreads throughout your body. It is like sunshine. You are filled with energy.

Very slowly take the light into your body. When you are rested and filled with energy, open your eyes. Sit up when you are ready.

Keep in touch with your body feelings.

If you pay attention to body messages,
you'll know when things are OK...
...are wrong...
...are the way you want them.

You can use your body energy...
to change things if you need to ... or
to enjoy things when they're OK.

Now

Take some time
to go over
what you have learned
about

Body 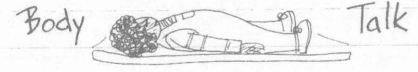 Talk

before you go on to the next part of the book.

Part 6

Letting Go

Some things get better when you let go...

...like...

a loose tooth...

 ...a hot pan...

When you love a puppy, mouse, or kitten, you let it go to be and to act like itself.

•Draw a picture of your favorite pet or one you would like to have.

It is good to learn to let go when you love someone.
So... you learn to let friends go...
to be... and to do...
what is important to them.

By allowing and letting go
of friends and loved ones,
you free them
to be themselves.

You can do things for
others and for yourself...
...because... you want to!

For instance... your friend can go to a
violin lesson while you go play baseball.

Your friend can have another friend...
and spend time with this friend without you.

Someone you love can be very different from
you and even like different things and still
be loved by you.

When your body is tight, letting go of the tightness feels good.

When your head hurts, you can relax and let go of the pain.

When you are afraid, saying it out loud helps to let it go.

When you are angry, saying, "I'm angry!" lets the anger out and can help it go away.

Let go of the idea that everyone
<u>has</u> to like you.

• Does the baker have
to like you to sell
you a cake?

• Does the doctor
have to like you to
treat your measles?

• Write down or draw some people you can work with who
don't have to like you.

Let go of the idea that
if someone doesn't like you,
you are bad... or you have failed.

Let go of the idea that in order to be liked you <u>have</u> to do what someone else wants you to do If you spend all your time doing what others want you to do ...

you never get a chance to be yourself!

A pretzel ⊘ person meets everyone's needs, tries to be liked by everyone, and does anything others want.

A pretzel ⊘ person has no opinions, no special likes or dislikes, and stretches to fit into whatever is happening.

A pretzel ⊘ person lets other people make decisions, like choosing the movie, the kind of birthday cake, the game to play, where to go and what to do.

Are you a pretzel person?
If so ... let go!

STOP being a pretzel person.
· by being who you are,
· by making decisions,
· by having opinions,
· by having likes and dislikes,
· by saying what you want and don't want.
It is OK to be you!

Let go of the idea that what you want
will come to you if you <u>wait</u>.

No one can read your mind.
<u>Ask</u> for what you want.

People who love you ... don't know...
what you're thinking.

Let them know.

Wishing is OK, ... but asking is faster.

Wanting is OK, and asking will get you what
you want more often...

like a hug... or... a birthday party

Let go of the idea that you can't ask for what
you want. (But don't expect to always get it).

- Write down or draw some of the things you would like to ask for.

Let go of the idea that men and boys have to be strong and can't cry, or can't show feelings, such as... fear or ...love or ... tenderness.

And...

let go of the idea that women and girls have to be weak and always cry and, have softer feelings, and can't take care of themselves.

Men, women, boys and girls are _all_ _human_.

We all have feelings.

We all can be... strong, or weak, or afraid or angry.

It is nice to be able to cry,

or feel sad,

or say you are scared,

or that you hurt,

or that you care.

And it is nice to be strong
and to help others.

It is nice to be human!

You can find your own strength and power.
You can learn what feels best to you.
You can let go and allow yourself to be,
and... you can

Like Yourself
and be your own good friend,

and

a good friend to others, too!

About Uplift Press

Uplift Press provides high quality, user-friendly, accessible materials that teach and uplift children and families. The ultimate goal of Liking Myself, The Mouse, the Monster and Me, and all of our future books, is preventing—through education—dysfunctional behaviors that cause social harm.

The Story of Uplift Press

Pat Palmer and Louise Hart became friends as graduate psychology students in Colorado, and both of their doctoral dissertations became best-selling books.

Pat's dissertation, on teaching assertiveness from an early age, was published as two children's books—*Liking Myself,* and *The Mouse, the Monster and Me.* They became international bestsellers in six languages, selling over half a million copies around the globe with Impact Publishers. They went out of print in the U.S. in 2000, much to the dismay of Louise's workshop participants. Copies were soon selling on Amazon for over a hundred dollars.

One day Louise's daughter, Kristen, found a hundred-year-old book in an antique store called *The Uplift Book of Child Culture.* The name became part of Louise's message to the world, and inspired her to become the new publisher for Pat's wonderful books.

Louise started a new career at age 70 to promote the good work of her 80 year old friend. Both feel their work will not be finished until all children are raised to believe in and understand themselves.

UPLIFT PRESS

www.upliftpress.com
888-415-3414
admin@upliftpress.com

About the Creators

Dr. Pat Palmer wrote many books for youngsters and adults. A clinical psychologist and former Director of the Assertiveness Training Institute in Denver, Dr. Palmer has always taken pleasure in teaching people to like themselves, stand up for themselves, and to be assertive with a smile and a kind manner. She also wrote *Teen Esteem* with Melissa Froehner to teach these and other skills to teens. In memory of her grandmother, who believed Pat could be anyone she wanted to be, she wrote *I Wish I Could Hold Your Hand* to help young people deal with losing a dear loved one. Dr. Pat Palmer continues to write at her home on Maui. Her books are especially popular in Japan as well as Germany, Spain, South Korea, China, Croatia, Denmark and the Philippines. Visit www.drpatpalmer.com to say hello.

Publisher **Dr. Louise Hart** is the author of two highly regarded books, *The Winning Family: Increasing Self-Esteem in Your Children and Yourself* and *On the Wings of Self Esteem*. Having presented workshops as far as Heidelberg, Moscow, Tokyo, and Okinawa, she now presents at conferences and in California's Bay Area. Learn more at www.drlouisehart.com and even watch her wonderful, informative presentations on parenting from home at www.youtube.com/drlouisehart.

Illustrator **Betty Shondeck**, a retired elementary school art teacher living in the Denver area, dusted off her pens for an update of these hand-crafted books for today's youngsters.

Kristen Caven co-founded Uplift Press, building the website and re-formatting Pat's updated books. Kristen's literary efforts can be enjoyed at www.kristencaven.com.

Download the free teacher's guides at www.upliftpress.com!

Other books by Pat Palmer:

THE MOUSE, THE MONSTER AND ME
by Pat Palmer, Ed.D.

Engaging artwork and exercises illustrate aggressive "monster" and passive "mouse" behaviors, helping young readers identify these characteristics in themselves and others This book explores the "me communication style, based on respects, rights, and responsibility, and teaches healthy, non-violent conflict management skills that help kids stop being - or attracting - bullies.

I WISH I COULD HOLD YOUR HAND
by Pat Palmer, Ed.D.

A best friend has moved away...Dad no longer lives with the family...a favorite relative or pet has died....
Loss can be traumatic for children. This warm and comforting book gently helps the grieving child understand his or her feelings--from denial and anger to guilt and sadness--and learn to accept and deal with them in healthy ways.

TEEN ESTEEM
A Self-Direction Manual for Young Adults
Pat Palmer, Ed.D., and Melissa Alberti Froehner

Without patronizing or lecturing, *Teen Esteem* helps teenagers develop the skills needed to handle peer pressure substance abuse, sexual expression, and more. *Teen Esteem* includes new material on being different, self-acceptance, cyber-bullying, and coping with depression --in oneself and in others.

Visit www.drpatpalmer.com for more information.

Recommended Reading:

THE WINNING FAMILY
by Dr. Louise Hart

A hopeful, engaging guide to positive parenting that focuses on the personal growth and development of parents along with their children. It offers a new, hopeful model for families where everyone can win.

Uniquely inspiring, accessible, and non-guilt-provoking!"
—Mothering Magazine

ON THE WINGS OF SELF-ESTEEM
by Dr. Louise Hart

An elegant little book that teaches about self-esteem: how it is lost, how to regain it, and how to keep it.

"A wonderful book! If everyone read this book and did the exercises, the pain and suffering we currently experience would disappear."
—Jack Canfield
co-author, *Chicken Soup for the Soul*

SELF-ESTEEM: THE BEST GIFT
Excerpt from *The Winning Family*

Download the eBook or order in bulk from www.drlouisehart.com

Available in English and Spanish.

Visit www.drlouisehart.com for more information.

Ordering Information

To order books by Pat Palmer or Louise Hart,
visit www.Amazon.com

Bookstores:
Contact 888-415-3414

Bulk orders for school districts, PTAs, churches, etc:
Contact 888-415-3414

www.upliftpress.com

Made in the USA